Stay on Top of Each Day

A Daily Planner

Activinotes

Activinotes
DAILY JOURNALS, PLANNERS, NOTEBOOKS AND OTHER BLANK BOOKS

DAILY PLANNER

DATE

M T W T F S S

Time	Activities for Today	Inspiration

LEARNINGS FOR THE DAY

REMINDERS FOR TOMORROW:

NOTES FOR THE DAY:

QUICK LIST

○
○
○
○
○
○
○
○
○

to go

contact

DAILY PLANNER

DATE

M T W T F S S

Time	Activities for Today	Inspiration

LEARNINGS FOR THE DAY

REMINDERS FOR TOMORROW:

NOTES FOR THE DAY:

QUICK LIST

to go	contact

DAILY PLANNER

DATE

M T W T F S S

Time	Activities for Today	Inspiration

LEARNINGS FOR THE DAY

REMINDERS FOR TOMORROW:

NOTES FOR THE DAY:

QUICK LIST

to go	contact

DAILY PLANNER

DATE _____

M T W T F S S

Time	Activities for Today	Inspiration

LEARNINGS FOR THE DAY

REMINDERS FOR TOMORROW:

NOTES FOR THE DAY:

QUICK LIST

to go

contact

DAILY PLANNER

DATE

M T W T F S S

Time	Activities for Today	Inspiration

LEARNINGS FOR THE DAY

REMINDERS FOR TOMORROW:

NOTES FOR THE DAY:

QUICK LIST

to go	contact

DAILY PLANNER

DATE

M   T   W   T   F   S   S

Time	Activities for Today	Inspiration

LEARNINGS FOR THE DAY

_____
_____
_____
_____

REMINDERS FOR TOMORROW:

_____
_____
_____
_____

NOTES FOR THE DAY:

_____
_____
_____
_____
_____
_____
_____
_____

QUICK LIST

to go	contact

DAILY PLANNER

M T W T F S S

Time	Activities for Today

Inspiration

LEARNINGS FOR THE DAY

REMINDERS FOR TOMORROW:

NOTES FOR THE DAY:

QUICK LIST

to go	contact

DAILY PLANNER

DATE

M T W T F S S

Time	Activities for Today	Inspiration

LEARNINGS FOR THE DAY

REMINDERS FOR TOMORROW:

NOTES FOR THE DAY:

QUICK LIST

	to go	contact

DAILY PLANNER

DATE

M T W T F S S

Time	Activities for Today	Inspiration

LEARNINGS FOR THE DAY

REMINDERS FOR TOMORROW:

NOTES FOR THE DAY:

QUICK LIST

to go

contact

DAILY PLANNER

DATE

M T W T F S S

Time	Activities for Today	Inspiration

LEARNINGS FOR THE DAY

REMINDERS FOR TOMORROW:

NOTES FOR THE DAY:

QUICK LIST

to go	contact

DAILY PLANNER

DATE

M T W T F S S

Time	Activities for Today

Inspiration

LEARNINGS FOR THE DAY

REMINDERS FOR TOMORROW:

NOTES FOR THE DAY:

QUICK LIST

to go

contact

DAILY PLANNER

DATE

M T W T F S S

Time	Activities for Today	Inspiration

LEARNINGS FOR THE DAY

REMINDERS FOR TOMORROW:

NOTES FOR THE DAY:

QUICK LIST

to go	contact

DAILY PLANNER

DATE

M T W T F S S

Time	Activities for Today	Inspiration

LEARNINGS FOR THE DAY

REMINDERS FOR TOMORROW:

NOTES FOR THE DAY:

QUICK LIST

○
○
○
○
○
○
○
○
○
○

to go	contact

DAILY PLANNER

DATE

| M | T | W | T | F | S | S |

Time	Activities for Today	Inspiration

LEARNINGS FOR THE DAY

REMINDERS FOR TOMORROW:

NOTES FOR THE DAY:

QUICK LIST

to go

contact

DAILY PLANNER

DATE

M T W T F S S

Time	Activities for Today

Inspiration

LEARNINGS FOR THE DAY

REMINDERS FOR TOMORROW:

NOTES FOR THE DAY:

QUICK LIST

to go

contact

DAILY PLANNER

DATE

M T W T F S S

Time	Activities for Today

Inspiration

LEARNINGS FOR THE DAY

REMINDERS FOR TOMORROW:

NOTES FOR THE DAY:

QUICK LIST

to go	contact

DAILY PLANNER

DATE

M T W T F S S

Time	Activities for Today

Inspiration

LEARNINGS FOR THE DAY

REMINDERS FOR TOMORROW:

NOTES FOR THE DAY:

QUICK LIST

to go	contact

DAILY PLANNER

DATE

M T W T F S S

Time	Activities for Today

Inspiration

LEARNINGS FOR THE DAY

REMINDERS FOR TOMORROW:

NOTES FOR THE DAY:

QUICK LIST

to go	contact

DAILY PLANNER

DATE

M T W T F S S

Time	Activities for Today

Inspiration

LEARNINGS FOR THE DAY

REMINDERS FOR TOMORROW:

NOTES FOR THE DAY:

QUICK LIST

to go

contact

DAILY PLANNER

DATE

M T W T F S S

Time	Activities for Today

Inspiration

LEARNINGS FOR THE DAY

REMINDERS FOR TOMORROW:

NOTES FOR THE DAY:

QUICK LIST

to go

contact

DAILY PLANNER

DATE

M T W T F S S

Time	Activities for Today	Inspiration

LEARNINGS FOR THE DAY

REMINDERS FOR TOMORROW:

NOTES FOR THE DAY:

QUICK LIST

to go	contact

Daily Planner

DATE

| M | T | W | T | F | S | S |

Time	Activities for Today	Inspiration

LEARNINGS FOR THE DAY

REMINDERS FOR TOMORROW:

NOTES FOR THE DAY:

QUICK LIST

to go	contact

Daily Planner

M T W T F S S

Time	Activities for Today

Inspiration

LEARNINGS FOR THE DAY

REMINDERS FOR TOMORROW:

NOTES FOR THE DAY:

QUICK LIST

to go	contact

DAILY PLANNER

DATE
M T W T F S S

Time	Activities for Today	Inspiration

LEARNINGS FOR THE DAY

REMINDERS FOR TOMORROW:

NOTES FOR THE DAY:

QUICK LIST

to go	contact

DAILY PLANNER

DATE

M T W T F S S

Time	Activities for Today	Inspiration

LEARNINGS FOR THE DAY

REMINDERS FOR TOMORROW:

NOTES FOR THE DAY:

QUICK LIST

to go	contact

DAILY PLANNER

DATE

M	T	W	T	F	S	S

Time	Activities for Today	Inspiration

LEARNINGS FOR THE DAY

REMINDERS FOR TOMORROW:

NOTES FOR THE DAY:

QUICK LIST

to go	contact

DAILY PLANNER

DATE

M T W T F S S

Time	Activities for Today	Inspiration

LEARNINGS FOR THE DAY

REMINDERS FOR TOMORROW:

NOTES FOR THE DAY:

QUICK LIST

to go	contact

DAILY PLANNER

DATE

M T W T F S S

Time	Activities for Today	Inspiration

LEARNINGS FOR THE DAY

REMINDERS FOR TOMORROW:

NOTES FOR THE DAY:

QUICK LIST

to go	contact

DAILY PLANNER

DATE

M	T	W	T	F	S	S

Time	Activities for Today	Inspiration

LEARNINGS FOR THE DAY

REMINDERS FOR TOMORROW:

NOTES FOR THE DAY:

QUICK LIST

○
○
○
○
○
○
○
○
○

to go	contact

DAILY PLANNER

DATE

M T W T F S S

Time	Activities for Today	Inspiration

LEARNINGS FOR THE DAY

REMINDERS FOR TOMORROW:

NOTES FOR THE DAY:

QUICK LIST

to go	contact

DAILY PLANNER

DATE

M T W T F S S

Time	Activities for Today	Inspiration

LEARNINGS FOR THE DAY

REMINDERS FOR TOMORROW:

NOTES FOR THE DAY:

QUICK LIST

○
○
○
○
○
○
○
○
○
○

to go

contact

DAILY PLANNER

DATE

M	T	W	T	F	S	S

Time	Activities for Today	Inspiration

LEARNINGS FOR THE DAY

REMINDERS FOR TOMORROW:

NOTES FOR THE DAY:

QUICK LIST

to go	contact

DAILY PLANNER

DATE

| | | | | | | |
|M|T|W|T|F|S|S|

Time	Activities for Today	Inspiration

LEARNINGS FOR THE DAY

REMINDERS FOR TOMORROW:

NOTES FOR THE DAY:

QUICK LIST

○
○
○
○
○
○
○
○
○

to go

contact

DAILY PLANNER

DATE

M T W T F S S

Time	Activities for Today	Inspiration

LEARNINGS FOR THE DAY

_____

_____

_____

REMINDERS FOR TOMORROW:

_____

_____

_____

NOTES FOR THE DAY:

_____

_____

_____

_____

_____

_____

QUICK LIST

○ _____
○ _____
○ _____
○ _____
○ _____
○ _____
○ _____
○ _____
○ _____

to go

contact

DAILY PLANNER

DATE

M T W T F S S

Time	Activities for Today

Inspiration

LEARNINGS FOR THE DAY

REMINDERS FOR TOMORROW:

NOTES FOR THE DAY:

QUICK LIST

	to go	contact

DAILY PLANNER

DATE

M T W T F S S

Time	Activities for Today	Inspiration

LEARNINGS FOR THE DAY

REMINDERS FOR TOMORROW:

NOTES FOR THE DAY:

QUICK LIST

to go	contact

DAILY PLANNER

DATE

M T W T F S S

Time	Activities for Today	Inspiration

LEARNINGS FOR THE DAY

REMINDERS FOR TOMORROW:

NOTES FOR THE DAY:

QUICK LIST

to go	contact

DAILY PLANNER

DATE

M T W T F S S

Time	Activities for Today	Inspiration

LEARNINGS FOR THE DAY

REMINDERS FOR TOMORROW:

NOTES FOR THE DAY:

QUICK LIST

to go	contact

DAILY PLANNER

DATE

M T W T F S S

Time	Activities for Today	Inspiration

LEARNINGS FOR THE DAY

REMINDERS FOR TOMORROW:

NOTES FOR THE DAY:

QUICK LIST

to go	contact

DAILY PLANNER

DATE

M T W T F S S

Time	Activities for Today	Inspiration

LEARNINGS FOR THE DAY

REMINDERS FOR TOMORROW:

NOTES FOR THE DAY:

QUICK LIST

to go	contact

DAILY PLANNER

DATE

M T W T F S S

Time	Activities for Today	Inspiration

LEARNINGS FOR THE DAY

REMINDERS FOR TOMORROW:

NOTES FOR THE DAY:

QUICK LIST

to go	contact

DAILY PLANNER

DATE

M T W T F S S

Time	Activities for Today	Inspiration

LEARNINGS FOR THE DAY

REMINDERS FOR TOMORROW:

NOTES FOR THE DAY:

QUICK LIST

to go	contact

DAILY PLANNER

DATE

M T W T F S S

Time	Activities for Today

Inspiration

LEARNINGS FOR THE DAY

REMINDERS FOR TOMORROW:

NOTES FOR THE DAY:

QUICK LIST

to go

contact

DAILY PLANNER

DATE

M T W T F S S

Time	Activities for Today	Inspiration

LEARNINGS FOR THE DAY

REMINDERS FOR TOMORROW:

NOTES FOR THE DAY:

QUICK LIST

to go

contact

DAILY PLANNER

DATE

M	T	W	T	F	S	S

Time	Activities for Today	Inspiration

LEARNINGS FOR THE DAY

REMINDERS FOR TOMORROW:

NOTES FOR THE DAY:

QUICK LIST

○
○
○
○
○
○
○
○
○

to go	contact

DAILY PLANNER

DATE

M T W T F S S

Time	Activities for Today	Inspiration

LEARNINGS FOR THE DAY

REMINDERS FOR TOMORROW:

NOTES FOR THE DAY:

QUICK LIST

to go	contact

DaILY PLaNNeR

DATE

M T W T F S S

Time	Activities for Today	Inspiration

LEARNINGS FOR THE DAY

REMINDERS FOR TOMORROW:

NOTES FOR THE DAY:

QUICK LIST

	to go	contact

DAILY PLANNER

DATE

M T W T F S S

Time	Activities for Today	Inspiration

LEARNINGS FOR THE DAY

REMINDERS FOR TOMORROW:

NOTES FOR THE DAY:

QUICK LIST

to go	contact

DAILY PLANNER

DATE

M T W T F S S

Time	Activities for Today	Inspiration

LEARNINGS FOR THE DAY

REMINDERS FOR TOMORROW:

NOTES FOR THE DAY:

QUICK LIST

to go	contact

DAILY PLANNER

DATE

M T W T F S S

Time	Activities for Today	Inspiration

LEARNINGS FOR THE DAY

REMINDERS FOR TOMORROW:

NOTES FOR THE DAY:

QUICK LIST

	to go	contact

Daily Planner

DATE

M T W T F S S

Time	Activities for Today	Inspiration

LEARNINGS FOR THE DAY

REMINDERS FOR TOMORROW:

NOTES FOR THE DAY:

QUICK LIST

to go	contact

DAILY PLANNER

DATE

| | | | | | | |

M T W T F S S

Time	Activities for Today	Inspiration

LEARNINGS FOR THE DAY

REMINDERS FOR TOMORROW:

NOTES FOR THE DAY:

QUICK LIST

to go	contact

DAILY PLANNER

DATE

M	T	W	T	F	S	S

Time	Activities for Today	Inspiration

LEARNINGS FOR THE DAY

REMINDERS FOR TOMORROW:

NOTES FOR THE DAY:

QUICK LIST

to go	contact

DAILY PLANNER

DATE

M	T	W	T	F	S	S

Time	Activities for Today

Inspiration

LEARNINGS FOR THE DAY

REMINDERS FOR TOMORROW:

NOTES FOR THE DAY:

QUICK LIST

○
○
○
○
○
○
○
○
○
○

to go

contact

DAILY PLANNER

DATE

M T W T F S S

Time	Activities for Today	Inspiration

LEARNINGS FOR THE DAY

REMINDERS FOR TOMORROW:

NOTES FOR THE DAY:

QUICK LIST

to go	contact

DAILY PLANNER

DATE

M T W T F S S

Time	Activities for Today

Inspiration

LEARNINGS FOR THE DAY

REMINDERS FOR TOMORROW:

NOTES FOR THE DAY:

QUICK LIST

to go

contact

DAILY PLANNER

M T W T F S S

Time	Activities for Today	Inspiration

LEARNINGS FOR THE DAY

REMINDERS FOR TOMORROW:

NOTES FOR THE DAY:

QUICK LIST

to go	contact

DAILY PLANNER

DATE

M T W T F S S

Time	Activities for Today	Inspiration

LEARNINGS FOR THE DAY

REMINDERS FOR TOMORROW:

NOTES FOR THE DAY:

QUICK LIST

to go	contact

DAILY PLANNER

DATE

M T W T F S S

Time	Activities for Today	Inspiration

LEARNINGS FOR THE DAY

REMINDERS FOR TOMORROW:

NOTES FOR THE DAY:

QUICK LIST

to go	contact

DAILY PLANNER

DATE

M T W T F S S

Time	Activities for Today

Inspiration

LEARNINGS FOR THE DAY

REMINDERS FOR TOMORROW:

NOTES FOR THE DAY:

QUICK LIST

to go

contact

DAILY PLANNER

DATE

M	T	W	T	F	S	S

Time	Activities for Today	Inspiration

LEARNINGS FOR THE DAY

REMINDERS FOR TOMORROW:

NOTES FOR THE DAY:

QUICK LIST

to go

contact

DAILY PLANNER

DATE

M T W T F S S

Time	Activities for Today	Inspiration

LEARNINGS FOR THE DAY

REMINDERS FOR TOMORROW:

NOTES FOR THE DAY:

QUICK LIST

to go	contact

DAILY PLANNER

DATE

M T W T F S S

Time	Activities for Today	Inspiration

LEARNINGS FOR THE DAY

REMINDERS FOR TOMORROW:

NOTES FOR THE DAY:

QUICK LIST

to go	contact

DAILY PLANNER

DATE

M T W T F S S

Time	Activities for Today	Inspiration

LEARNINGS FOR THE DAY

REMINDERS FOR TOMORROW:

NOTES FOR THE DAY:

QUICK LIST

to go	contact

DAILY PLANNER

DATE

M	T	W	T	F	S	S

Time	Activities for Today	Inspiration

LEARNINGS FOR THE DAY

REMINDERS FOR TOMORROW:

NOTES FOR THE DAY:

QUICK LIST

○
○
○
○
○
○
○
○
○
○

to go

contact

DAILY PLANNER

DATE

| | | | | | | |
|M|T|W|T|F|S|S|

Time	Activities for Today

Inspiration

LEARNINGS FOR THE DAY

REMINDERS FOR TOMORROW:

NOTES FOR THE DAY:

QUICK LIST

to go	contact

DAILY PLANNER

DATE

M T W T F S S

Time	Activities for Today	Inspiration

LEARNINGS FOR THE DAY

REMINDERS FOR TOMORROW:

NOTES FOR THE DAY:

QUICK LIST

to go	contact

DAILY PLANNER

DATE

M T W T F S S

Time	Activities for Today	Inspiration

LEARNINGS FOR THE DAY

REMINDERS FOR TOMORROW:

NOTES FOR THE DAY:

QUICK LIST

to go	contact

DAILY PLANNER

DATE

M T W T F S S

Time	Activities for Today	Inspiration

LEARNINGS FOR THE DAY

REMINDERS FOR TOMORROW:

NOTES FOR THE DAY:

QUICK LIST

	to go	contact

DAILY PLANNER

DATE

M	T	W	T	F	S	S

Time	Activities for Today	Inspiration

LEARNINGS FOR THE DAY

REMINDERS FOR TOMORROW:

NOTES FOR THE DAY:

QUICK LIST

to go	contact

DAILY PLANNER

DATE

M T W T F S S

Time	Activities for Today	Inspiration

LEARNINGS FOR THE DAY

REMINDERS FOR TOMORROW:

NOTES FOR THE DAY:

QUICK LIST

○
○
○
○
○
○
○
○
○

to go

contact

DAILY PLANNER

DATE

M T W T F S S

Time	Activities for Today	Inspiration

LEARNINGS FOR THE DAY

REMINDERS FOR TOMORROW:

NOTES FOR THE DAY:

QUICK LIST

to go	contact

DAILY PLANNER

DATE

M T W T F S S

Time	Activities for Today

Inspiration

LEARNINGS FOR THE DAY

REMINDERS FOR TOMORROW:

NOTES FOR THE DAY:

QUICK LIST

to go

contact

DAILY PLANNER

DATE

M T W T F S S

Time	Activities for Today	Inspiration

LEARNINGS FOR THE DAY

REMINDERS FOR TOMORROW:

NOTES FOR THE DAY:

QUICK LIST

to go	contact

DAILY PLANNER

DATE

M T W T F S S

Time	Activities for Today	Inspiration

LEARNINGS FOR THE DAY

REMINDERS FOR TOMORROW:

NOTES FOR THE DAY:

QUICK LIST

to go

contact

DAILY PLANNER

DATE

M T W T F S S

Time	Activities for Today

Inspiration

LEARNINGS FOR THE DAY

REMINDERS FOR TOMORROW:

NOTES FOR THE DAY:

QUICK LIST

to go	contact

DAILY PLANNER

DATE

M T W T F S S

Time	Activities for Today

Inspiration

LEARNINGS FOR THE DAY

REMINDERS FOR TOMORROW:

NOTES FOR THE DAY:

QUICK LIST

to go

contact

DAILY PLANNER

DATE

☐ ☐ ☐ ☐ ☐ ☐ ☐
M T W T F S S

Time	Activities for Today

Inspiration

_____
_____
_____
_____
_____
_____
_____
_____
_____
_____
_____
_____
_____
_____
_____

LEARNINGS FOR THE DAY

_____
_____
_____
_____

REMINDERS FOR TOMORROW:

_____
_____
_____
_____

NOTES FOR THE DAY:

_____
_____
_____
_____
_____
_____
_____
_____
_____

QUICK LIST

○ _____
○ _____
○ _____
○ _____
○ _____
○ _____
○ _____
○ _____
○ _____
○ _____

to go	contact

DAILY PLANNER

DATE

M T W T F S S

Time	Activities for Today	Inspiration

LEARNINGS FOR THE DAY

REMINDERS FOR TOMORROW:

NOTES FOR THE DAY:

QUICK LIST

	to go	contact

DAILY PLANNER

DATE

M T W T F S S

Time	Activities for Today

Inspiration

LEARNINGS FOR THE DAY

REMINDERS FOR TOMORROW:

NOTES FOR THE DAY:

QUICK LIST

to go

contact

DAILY PLANNER

DATE

M	T	W	T	F	S	S

Time	Activities for Today	Inspiration

LEARNINGS FOR THE DAY

REMINDERS FOR TOMORROW:

NOTES FOR THE DAY:

QUICK LIST

to go	contact

DAILY PLANNER

DATE

M T W T F S S

Time	Activities for Today	Inspiration

LEARNINGS FOR THE DAY

REMINDERS FOR TOMORROW:

NOTES FOR THE DAY:

QUICK LIST

to go	contact

DAILY PLANNER

DATE

M T W T F S S

Time	Activities for Today	Inspiration

LEARNINGS FOR THE DAY

REMINDERS FOR TOMORROW:

NOTES FOR THE DAY:

QUICK LIST

to go	contact

DAILY PLANNER

DATE

M T W T F S S

Time	Activities for Today

Inspiration

LEARNINGS FOR THE DAY

REMINDERS FOR TOMORROW:

NOTES FOR THE DAY:

QUICK LIST

to go

contact

DAILY PLANNER

DATE

M T W T F S S

Time	Activities for Today	Inspiration

LEARNINGS FOR THE DAY

REMINDERS FOR TOMORROW:

NOTES FOR THE DAY:

QUICK LIST

○
○
○
○
○
○
○
○
○

to go	contact

DAILY PLANNER

DATE

M T W T F S S

Time	Activities for Today	Inspiration

LEARNINGS FOR THE DAY

REMINDERS FOR TOMORROW:

NOTES FOR THE DAY:

QUICK LIST

○
○
○
○
○
○
○
○
○

to go

contact

DAILY PLANNER

DATE

M T W T F S S

Time	Activities for Today

Inspiration

LEARNINGS FOR THE DAY

REMINDERS FOR TOMORROW:

NOTES FOR THE DAY:

QUICK LIST

to go

contact

DAILY PLANNER

DATE

M T W T F S S

Time	Activities for Today	Inspiration

LEARNINGS FOR THE DAY

REMINDERS FOR TOMORROW:

NOTES FOR THE DAY:

QUICK LIST

to go	contact

DAILY PLANNER

DATE

| M | T | W | T | F | S | S |

Time	Activities for Today	Inspiration

LEARNINGS FOR THE DAY

REMINDERS FOR TOMORROW:

NOTES FOR THE DAY:

QUICK LIST

to go	contact

DAILY PLANNER

DATE

| | | | | | | |
|M|T|W|T|F|S|S|

Time	Activities for Today	Inspiration

LEARNINGS FOR THE DAY

REMINDERS FOR TOMORROW:

NOTES FOR THE DAY:

QUICK LIST

to go	contact

DAILY PLANNER

DATE
| | | | | | | |
|M|T|W|T|F|S|S|

Time	Activities for Today	Inspiration

LEARNINGS FOR THE DAY

REMINDERS FOR TOMORROW:

NOTES FOR THE DAY:

QUICK LIST

to go	contact

DAILY PLANNER

DATE

M T W T F S S

Time	Activities for Today	Inspiration

LEARNINGS FOR THE DAY

REMINDERS FOR TOMORROW:

NOTES FOR THE DAY:

QUICK LIST

to go	contact

DAILY PLANNER

DATE

M T W T F S S

Time	Activities for Today	Inspiration

LEARNINGS FOR THE DAY

REMINDERS FOR TOMORROW:

NOTES FOR THE DAY:

QUICK LIST

○
○
○
○
○
○
○
○
○
○

to go	contact

DAILY PLANNER

DATE

M T W T F S S

Time	Activities for Today	Inspiration

LEARNINGS FOR THE DAY

REMINDERS FOR TOMORROW:

NOTES FOR THE DAY:

QUICK LIST

to go	contact

DAILY PLANNER

DATE

M T W T F S S

Time	Activities for Today	Inspiration

LEARNINGS FOR THE DAY

_____
_____
_____
_____

REMINDERS FOR TOMORROW:

_____
_____
_____
_____

NOTES FOR THE DAY:

_____
_____
_____
_____
_____
_____
_____
_____

QUICK LIST

	to go	contact

DAILY PLANNER

DATE

M T W T F S S

Time	Activities for Today	Inspiration

LEARNINGS FOR THE DAY

REMINDERS FOR TOMORROW:

NOTES FOR THE DAY:

QUICK LIST

to go	contact

DAILY PLANNER

DATE

M T W T F S S

Time	Activities for Today	Inspiration

LEARNINGS FOR THE DAY

REMINDERS FOR TOMORROW:

NOTES FOR THE DAY:

QUICK LIST

to go	contact

DAILY PLANNER

DATE

| M | T | W | T | F | S | S |

Time	Activities for Today	Inspiration

LEARNINGS FOR THE DAY

REMINDERS FOR TOMORROW:

NOTES FOR THE DAY:

QUICK LIST

to go	contact

DAILY PLANNER

DATE

M T W T F S S

Time	Activities for Today	Inspiration

LEARNINGS FOR THE DAY

REMINDERS FOR TOMORROW:

NOTES FOR THE DAY:

QUICK LIST

to go	contact

Daily Planner

DATE

M T W T F S S

Time	Activities for Today	Inspiration

LEARNINGS FOR THE DAY

REMINDERS FOR TOMORROW:

NOTES FOR THE DAY:

QUICK LIST

to go

contact

DAILY PLANNER

DATE

M	T	W	T	F	S	S

Time	Activities for Today	Inspiration

LEARNINGS FOR THE DAY

REMINDERS FOR TOMORROW:

NOTES FOR THE DAY:

QUICK LIST

to go	contact

DAILY PLANNER

DATE

M T W T F S S

Time	Activities for Today	Inspiration

LEARNINGS FOR THE DAY

REMINDERS FOR TOMORROW:

NOTES FOR THE DAY:

QUICK LIST

to go	contact

DAILY PLANNER

DATE

| M | T | W | T | F | S | S |

Time	Activities for Today	Inspiration

LEARNINGS FOR THE DAY

REMINDERS FOR TOMORROW:

NOTES FOR THE DAY:

QUICK LIST

	to go	contact

DAILY PLANNER

DATE

M T W T F S S

Time	Activities for Today

Inspiration

LEARNINGS FOR THE DAY

REMINDERS FOR TOMORROW:

NOTES FOR THE DAY:

QUICK LIST

○
○
○
○
○
○
○
○
○
○

to go

contact

www.ingramcontent.com/pod-product-compliance
Lightning Source LLC
Chambersburg PA
CBHW080737250626
47170CB00010B/2864